Book of Snark

Book of Snark

Wit & Wisdom for the Angry
Professional Woman on the Bus

Tension Mounts

ISBN: 979-8-6880-7688-2
Book of Snark Copyright © 2020 C.M.Mounts

Cover design by Alexander Niece
alexnie.myportfolio.com

For Bill & Mary--
All my love to you, mom & dad...
Sorry you are not here to be embarrassed!

Welcome to the Book of Snark
If you read it, you have no one to blame but yourself.

Cube Farm

The worst place to get lunch has
got to be the staff refrigerator.

Working Girl

Monday morning is that time when the week already royally sucks and you are not at work yet.

Living that high-profile glamorous lifestyle that only an office job can provide.

1oz of ambition is worth 10oz of intelligence and they will hate you if you have both.

Repeat frequently: I can, I can, I can (but really, should I?)

Career Options

I work here only because vigilante was not a viable career choice.

Well, the good news is that I am probably not getting laid off. The bad news is that I am probably not getting laid off.

Here's to having a job so boring no one ever wants to talk to you about it!

Every industry had its corruptions. Figure out what you can tolerate, then pick your devil and dance with it.

Team Player

Being a specific person, I sometimes find it difficult to work with people in general.

It's not good to be popular at work because you will get assigned to the hard jobs first.

If you really want to see it done, just do the work and stop worrying about who gets the fucking credit.

Working Too Much

You know you have been working too much
when you have no idea what day it is and forgot
you got paid two days ago.

You know it's a hard day when the boss says,
"Please come back tomorrow" as they leave for
the night.

You know it's a long day when you come home
from work, fall into bed with your winter boots
on, and pass out for an hour.

Motivation

I am still at work and there is no beer.

Quick! Someone drive by my house and run me over as I cross the street to the bus stop, so I have an excuse to not go to work!

The only thing keeping me going these days is Led Zeppelin and vending machine coffee.

Work always sucks until I remember what life would be like if I were unemployed.

Overtime

How many work hours does it take until you feel like you are going to puke?

When you lock yourself out of the office where your purse, car keys, cell phone, blasting radio, and data crunching computer are located, stop working.

Friendly reminder: Your employer will not stop you from working yourself into an early grave if you choose to do that.

Time Off

It takes so little time to crush the vacation right out of you.

The minute I don't have work to keep me regulated I revert right back into a shiftless night dweller.

The problem with taking vacation is that all those projects are still waiting for you when you get back but now you have less time to complete them.

And with the first day back after vacation comes the inevitable, "OK, wait- what the hell do I do for a living?"

Office Life

Oh, all-seeing electronic plumbing eye… you are not capable of making better decisions than I am.

Is there a stronger ipecac than walking into the office?

PSA: If you are white and work in an office please refrain from referring to anything being 'my jam' or 'not my jam' besides incidents involving the copier or printer.

Which is less painful: Annual employee review or dental check-up?

It is no easy task to spend 1/3 of your life on a hamster wheel.

Lunchroom

You're having lunch in a funky little bistro. I'm having lunch in the office breakroom which offers a different kind of funk.

Someone in the work lunchroom sarcastically teased me about secretly being a 'vulgar comedian'. I told him to check with me in my off hours.

As a co-worker retrieved his lunch from the staff refrigerator, he could see the hole where someone else had eaten part of his sandwich. The would-be thief took one bite, decided he didn't like it, and put it back. There was a moment when he considered his options, whether to line up the imprint with everyone's teeth, but he threw it away and left the lunchroom.

Weekend

And the end of workday Friday hits like a brick...

I believe the real reason it is called Friday is because we are all fried by the time it ends.

Welcome to the weekend and remember all those people that worked and died in insane factory conditions to make it all possible for you.

Fuck. We all have to get up for work on Monday.

Working Schlub

There is nothing wrong with the software
other than the way you are using it.

IT Help Desk

Help Desk Mambo: a dance where you try to ask someone "what the bloody hell are you talking about" without making them feel dumb.

Turns out that just because you want access doesn't mean you get access.

It is sad that being efficient confuses people and makes them nervous.

PMS help desk isn't.

User Error

No software in the world can make up for your basic computer illiteracy.

If you do not know how to navigate to a website, do not blame any software for any reason.

Some people are abusive to help desk professionals and usually when the problem is user error.

SELECT * FROM users WHERE clue > 0

Difficult Customers

So, why don't you ask a question instead of
monkey punching things you don't understand?

If you didn't tell me you needed it, you do not
get to be mad about it.

Just because you do not know what we are
doing does not mean we do not know what we
are doing.

Email

It is a very simple thing to type 'ass' instead of 'add' in a work email. The spell checker will not catch it.

Please do not sign your emails with the valediction of 'Best' because it sounds really fucking plastic and I hate you.

I am so thrilled to write out directions and email them to you about how to fix your problem so that you don't read them and call me to complain instead!

If you received an email from me, I did not send it because I don't love you the way spambots do.

Meetings

I love meetings where fights almost break out.

Meetings only serve to prevent you from getting work done while assigning you more work.

There comes a point when the details matter and those who consistently say, "We'll figure it out later" never realize that right now is in fact later.

Communications

I am going to re-record my voicemail to just say "Cram it!"

I probably shouldn't use the phrase 'go to hell' in conjunction with my work.

Is it wrong for me to announce that something related to work politics is 'bullshit' in a staff meeting?

I detest 'business speak'. Just fucking say what you mean and mean what you say without trying to use the word 'synergy'.

Training & Presentations

I was sent to conflict fluency training presumably so I can be more fluent in conflict.

I have to do a presentation this morning. I hope no one shows up.

I am not sure why I thought conducting a training after a dental appointment was a good idea but here we are.

If there is anything better than giving a presentation at a conference for work on a Sunday afternoon, I don't know what it is.

Have Fare, Will Travel

Dear bus weirdo: I know we haven't seen each other in six months but we are not old friends.

Cars

Why am I not as thrilled to be a member of AAA as the lady in the advertisement?

Turns out that when you drive a car you are encased in glass. We can all see you core out your nostril and it looks like you are shoving a wooden dowel perpendicular into your face.

If I put the car in drive and let it roll off a cliff, will they forgive the loan so I can go out and get a different car?

I want to know the percentage of people that have driven around naked. Is it a lot or just me?

Bus Stop

Every bus stop comes with three people who have nothing to say but refuse to shut up.

Living the glamour of big city life by eating dinner out of a box, while waiting on a bus to take me home.

The high frequency 'Downtown' bus when you are not going downtown is really fucking unhelpful.

I need to find a bus stop that won't endanger my life because it is rammed by cars, who don't see the large steel and glass box, as they turn the corner.

Get on the Bus

Hot coffee facial splash & dash- now available
on all city buses!

I am on the bus asking myself why I am on the
bus.

The fact that we both have umbrellas and ride
the same bus does not reveal some deep kinship
between us.

To the hipster chick trying to look all frosty on
the bus: you farted and I know it.

If I've learned anything on the express bus, it's
that major pencil-necked science geeks love to
rock out.

Alternative Transportation

It is now time to catch the bus that will take me to the train that goes to the airport and pick up my rental car.

Is there anything more pleasant than being stuck in a train car with a drunk screaming baby shower?

The cab from the airport smells like cat pee but maybe it's the driver.

Whenever I hear of gridlock during a mandatory evacuation, I remember that I ride a long-distance touring bicycle and all is well.

I still think purchasing a Zamboni for my winter commutes to work is a good idea.

Airplanes

It is in the airlines best interest to make economy class as shitty as they think most people will accept without causing a riot in order to drive people that can afford it to more expensive seats.

I am ever so pissed I will not be allowed to bring my cattle prod in my carry-on bag.

I once had an Englishman, clearly weary from international travel, refuse to sit in the same row with me because he assumed I was a plump mid-western bumpkin and therefore would not be interesting to talk to. Your loss, dumb ass.

Well, yesterday included among other things an emergency landing at O'hare due to the 82-year-old man three rows up who died and came back to life. Whelp, off to today's adventure!

FYI: The crash probably won't kill you, but the resultant jet fueled fireball will. You're welcome.

Home Sweet Home

You know you've been moving when the prize you find in the cereal box is a marker.

Moving

How do I tell a prospective landlord that the
last place I lived burned down.

What could be more fun than sorting and
packing without A/C on a hellish July day?

Things that you are not required to move:
stacks of unread magazines; unfinished craft
projects you promised yourself to finish after
the previous move; the old mop and stinky
trash can (buy new ones).

There is the hassle of moving the crap, then the
hassle of figuring out where the crap goes.
Perhaps it would all look best at the city dump.

Gas Company

Monday morning is not the time to find the pilot light is out on the water heater.

Gas leak, no heat. Not me, my house.

I mean, if the heat is out, and you have to go to the to store to buy a space heater, during the first significant snow fall of the season, you might as well splurge and get the remote-control 'fireplace'.

Gnawed up cow bone dog treats are a great way to scare the gasman.

Home Improvement

Who wants a new car when you can rewire your entire house for the same price?

I want to install a robotic chicken sandwich maker in my home for no damn reason.

January is a great time for large home organization projects but your house will look like the closets exploded.

PSA: Do not carpet your walls, kitchen, bathroom, or van.

Household Chores

I really should just burn this laundry.

I have been cleaning my apartment all
afternoon and will now enjoy the five minutes it
stays that way.

Robotic vacuum cleaners seem like a good idea
until the dog has diarrhea.

What sort of monster mows the fucking lawn at
7am?

Household Accidents

I fell down in front of the door to my building as I watched the maintenance guy try to figure out how to use the salt spreader.

Helpful tips that make things worse are not helpful.

I went on vacation for two weeks upon my return discovered mushrooms growing out of the bathroom radiator.

Neighborhood

With super soaker in hand, I am now prepared
to deal with the alley cat that attaches itself to
my kitchen window.

When I grow up, I want to sit on my front
porch and needle complete strangers about their
parking skills.

I am sorry dude sleeping on the ratty balcony
couch. I did not mean to wake you on my way
to work.

I thought the people across the street were
watching porn, but it was PBS.

If there's anything more relaxing than listening
to someone vacuum their car during dinner, I
can't think of what it might be.

Shop Until You Drop

There are certain lines I will not cross and buying used underwear is one of them.

Questionable Goods

Many people probably won't buy ham on clearance marked 'AS IS' but I did because I like to live dangerously.

The major problem with certain bath tissue is crotch lint. Nobody wants or needs crotch lint.

I want to know why the most expensive furniture is also the ugliest.

Mouthwash was once marketed as a floor cleaner and treatment for gonorrhea because, hey, oral sex.*

Color coordinating your toilet paper to your bathroom goes too far.

*Not medically accurate

Do What You Gotta To Do

No toilet paper... goodbye socks.

Carrying kitty litter on the bus is not as light and fluffy as the kitty on the bag.

I have no air conditioning in the house, so I am going to go grocery shopping and browse the frozen vegetable section for about two hours.

You can wash dishes with shampoo in a pinch, but I would avoid washing your hair with dish soap.

Shopping

It's not a bargain if it's hideous.

If you like corporate America's white-washed, cookie cutter offerings designed for the lowest common denominator please ignore this message: Support your local businesses and artisans!

Shopping on Saturday night is always best because everyone else is out having fun.

I am quite sure the gates of hell can be found at deep discounts within your area Big Box store.

Women's Fashion

If you choose to wear heels, please learn to walk in them.

Overheard, dressing room: "There's just nothing I can do about the romper crotch area"

Are exercise pants the only ones you are allowed to wear as high waters?

I want to know if anyone else has experienced an increase in 'hem blowout'. All my new pants and sweaters have lost their hems. I think I know where clothing manufacturers are cutting costs... We need more hem, less haw.

Fashion Faux Pas

I am bringing back sexy in my snow boots and dress pants.

I sincerely wish make-up was my biggest problem.

At least my pants are long enough to cover up the fact that I am wearing two different socks.

I think anyone that cannot pick out clothes that make them look good should be prohibited from picking out their own tattoos.

While I dressed for the summer weather, on reflection I realize that woodland sprites picked out my outfit.

Food & Drink

But what if I WANT to eat the freshness packet?

Fruits & Vegetables

Asparagus for breakfast is the bacon of the forest.

Truffles not trifles!

Prunes get a bum rap.

Who says Brussels sprouts aren't road food?

Overheard, December: "The quality of the blueberries here is terrible and it's so expensive!" Really?

Junk Food

I want a dietary warning label on the side of all junk food that reads: "This product contains everything you already know is bad for you so just shut up and eat it!"

There are times when cheese puffs and chocolate milk seem like a viable dinner choice.

Turns out black licorice can kill you. I guess that's why it tastes like death.

It's a cheese, Chardonnay, and cookies kind of night.

Inedible

I used to keep a glass of water by my bed and sip from it during the night until I found a spider floating in it.

The moment you look in the fridge after putting the cereal in the bowl and remember you are out of milk.

All water has been pissed out of some creature at some point in time.

I'm celebrating Earth Day by eating fast food.

Wine

Emergency! My wine key is missing!

I just heard that the greatest risk to a dinner party is running out of wine. They've obviously never eaten at my house.

Wine and furniture assembly. A winning combination.

Am I bougie if I own a white wine koozie?

Why I Drink Coffee

I gave up cigarettes... I will not give up coffee if
for no other reason than public safety.

I left work and bought a coffee because they
frown on sleeping at your desk.

The coffee vending machine blinked 'winner',
returned my money, and dispensed a free cup of
coffee.

There is no 'X' in espresso.

Coffee Nightmares

Coffee and toothpaste are not a good flavor combination.

The peppermint flavored coffee was on clearance. Why did I think that was a good enough reason.

Imagine my horror when I realized on Monday morning that the coffee I bought was decaf.

Every time I come to this coffee shop I remember why I don't come to this coffee shop.

There is only so much coffee can fix.

The Internet

It turns out that the Internet is not the place
to find peace and happiness.

My Brain on Social Media

I'm not social enough to be any good at social media.

My social media was so much more insightful before I stopped giving a shit.

In 2010, I often posted philosophic reflections on social media. In 2020, toilet humor.

And all this time, I was supposed to punctuate my snarky remarks with a winky face. ;)

So very tired but not so much I can't go online and bitch about it.

Your Brain on Social Media

Frankly, I do not care what is 'trending' because most people are ambulance chasing morons.

Social media often appears like an angry mob with torches and pitchforks.

Hey everybody! Let's all obsess over rude comments from strangers since there is nothing else going on in the world...

Only Mr. Spock's death could end the great white dress-blue dress debate of 2015.

Random Thoughts

Does anyone else think it's weird that chain mail became chain emails and are now chain statuses?

The feed hides my posts about my writing in an effort to get me to pay to promote my free writing to my family and friends.

Some video uploads sound like they come from a very warped and worn cassette played back under water.

WWW

I tried to Google map 'Home Depot' but instead typed in 'Hoe Depot'. The first location it suggested was the football stadium. Well played Google.

I think that any internet service that is so damn slow that you cannot send a simple email is not so much an ISP as a POS.

The Internet has made life easier for everybody including scoundrels.

Does anyone else remember when Amazon was just an online bookstore that eventually went bankrupt? Apparently, they reorganized.

Shut It Off

Merry Christmas poor electronic replacement for real human connection!!!

Hey everybody! How about we delete our online profiles and go get a God damn cup of coffee!

Think about what you could accomplish if you stopped spending time online and focused on the one great passion of your life... Hmm... Bye!

Idiot Box

I like my news with a little less WWE flair.

TV

Sorry folks but when you say, "I don't watch TV, I do Netflix" it's the same fucking thing.

People become visibly uncomfortable if no, you really don't want to watch TV.

Your need to rush home to watch your television show does not constitute an emergency.

Marketing

It's ok. We know how hard thinking for yourself is. Let us do it for you. You'll thank us later. -The American Marketing Association.

Marketing departments that apply highly dramatic music to mundane and everyday activities and products drive me to not watch their advertising. Good job.

Dear weatherman: I am sorry your job is boring but cut the fucking hype and just deliver the weather.

Sports

Who knew that organ music could make baseball so much more exciting.

Do you picture the timpani player on the Olympic theme song as a burly, oily man draped in a ragged toga? You do now...

The reason that men's golf pants come in horrible patterns is so that if the guy has a heart attack, they can find the body in the rough.

The News

I have come full circle to getting my news from the newspaper because I would rather read in silence than listen to some idiot yapping their innuendos and opinions at me.

The less people understand, the more insane they behave. Tell me again why basic global literacy is not a priority.

If folks would stop sitting around with a presumptive attitude that they are knowledgeable about everything and actually spent some time ensuring that they were actually knowledgeable about something, we all would be in a lot better place.
At least, I assume so.

Government

I read the Constitution for the articles.

You do know that they financially constrain non-commercial artists as a form of censorship, right?

U.S. out of Nebraska!

Remember when the government didn't act like it was run by drug addicts? Those were the days!

Voting

Hey assholes! It's mid-term elections in one week so get out the vote you lazy... oh never mind.

OK everybody, try not to barf on your ballot and be sure to wash your hands when you are done.

Honest bumper stickers: "I pick my nose and I vote."; "I eat cheese and I vote."; "I think my wife smells funny and I vote."; "I lie about being good at things and I vote."

If as a candidate you call yourself 'Danger Ron', how the hell do you expect to be taken seriously?

People complain that the dead vote in Chicago but seriously, why would they bother?

Politics

Don't forget to tune into the 'State of the Onion' address tonight to see what stinks.

Have you ever noticed the percentage of pictures of women in positions of power used by the media that depict them shrieking? It's a lot.

Explain to me- why are so many people's identity and ego tied to politicians and political parties?

FYI: You can make a fortune telling people what they want to hear.

General Public

The general public is really just the general pubic.

Shut Up

Can everyone please stop calling ordinary things 'amazing'?

I think the world needs more kids' movies where everyone is a smartass. That will work out just fine.

It is sometimes difficult to be an auditory learner among those whose attention seeking behavior is expressed by voluble inane prattle.

PSA: Nobody gives a shit about your dietary restrictions so please avoid it when you are searching for topics of conversation.

If your primary mode of communication is whining, please shut the hell up.

Not Funny

Turns out I offend people. I really don't know what the fuck their problem is.

Just because you think you have a sense of humor does not mean you have to inflict it on the rest of us.

There is a distinct difference between being funny and being an asshole but most don't know what it is.

Try Something Different

What a luxury it is to get uptight about shit that absolutely does not matter.

Try doing the opposite of what you would normally do and see what happens. As an aside, I don't answer phone calls from jail.

Are you doing the most you can to make other people's lives miserable? Fucking stop it.

Folks, please stop shortening the word 'analysis' to 'anal', even though that's what analysis requires.

If you are tempted to pump someone you barely know for information regarding their personal life or trauma, resist this temptation.

Crowds

I am an extrovert that doesn't like people. The struggle is real.

When I go out to crowded events, I am reminded why I don't go out to crowded events.

Be there or be... whatever really...

Strangers

I am sorry that you are mental, but I did not
cause you to be that way.

There is always some woman on the telephone
screaming at some man in front of the
downtown central library.

Big Box discount stores are full of unhappy
people. So is the casino.

Yes, I do provide professional help but not of
the kind you need.

You can squeeze the information out of her,
but I have got to warn you, she's gassy.

Misunderstood

Just because you say it doesn't make it true.

I ask you to consider the many people who have the wrong impression of you when you make your assessment of others.

Those with honor are frequently misunderstood by those without it.

When you give a positive comment to those who are conditioned to hear only negative comments there is always a pause in conversation while they scan for the absent insult.

Unreasonable Expectations

We waste a lot of energy hating and criticizing ourselves for that which we have no power to change.

If you rely on others to ensure that your experience of life is a positive one, you will be sorely disappointed.

It is a baffling human habit to feed off the accomplishments or drama of others.

The world is full of people that hate themselves. Look at the state of it.

Are you just barely hanging on to self and sanity? So are most of the people on this planet.

Brotherly Love

The younger generations have absolutely no idea how much the older generations love them until they themselves become the older generations.

It is never wrong to care about others. The danger only lies in caring for them.

There is a place for us all if we are willing to make room for us all.

Hey you! Get outside and enjoy yourself so much this weekend that someone tries to steal you!

40+ SWF

I know a woman is expected to know
her place but I clearly do not.

Career Woman

The woman just sat down and fucking did it.

If you are an intelligent independent woman with strong opinions, prepare yourself to be attacked by society at large.

Not all women with careers are career driven.

Being a bitch and being a strong woman are not the same thing.

If you do not like the design then take it up with the designer.

Middle Age

Tolerance for bullshit currently at punk rock level.

I am living life not so much in the fast lane as the construction zone.

Lord, age me to a fine wine... not strong vinegar.

Men have no idea how hard it is for a woman to wash her crotch.

That moment you go to the doctor excited about how much weight you've lost and he tells you to lose weight.

Early to Bed

I drank a cup of coffee and immediately took a nap.

I took an hour nap and now I am ready for bed.

I got ready to go out and ended up asleep on the couch.

PMS

Today I am grateful that panty liners make it so that I am free to be me.

I shall rampage the city like Godzilla and kill and kill until someone fires chocolate bullets into my mouth!

OK, maybe talking to my boss while I have PMS was not the greatest idea.

Aren't they really more like horror-mones?

Home Entertainment

I am spending Friday night cleaning out my
inbox.

It's going to be another wild night of playing
fetch with the cat.

I will sew a patch on all my clothing that reads
'No Fun'.

Who says single women and jazz music rarely
mix?

Chores

Spent the evening scouring the kitchen island.
You're jealous.

Sunday night is a great time to watch fruit flies
drown in vinegar.

You know you are officially bored out of your
skull when you look forward to cleaning the cat
box.

Living it up in the big city. Time to do laundry.

Food Therapy

I need a great big bear hug but am settling for beer and pizza.

I opted to go get an ice cream sandwich instead of tearing my hair out.

Drinking beer before grocery shopping is an OK idea, right?

God how I wish I'd actually smashed my face into that cake. You only regret the things you don't do.

I got two prizes in my Cracker Jack. Things are looking up.

Style

Being a guest at a wedding probably requires me to wash up a little.

Hair is cut and I feel the need to strut.

Only one good thing about this hot humid weather- my naturals curls look great!

Nothing makes a person uglier than a sneer.

What we trade in physical beauty, we gain in spiritual beauty.

Benefits

No one to spend Valentine's with? Guess this bottle of wine is all for me!

I forgot what single life could be like. Nobody waiting at home tapping their watch!

Strangely, everything remains exactly where I left it.

Get Yourself Out There!

I would rather do it alone than not do it at all.
No, not that.

Life is too short to wait for someone to buy you
flowers.

Why do people look at a woman eating dinner
alone like she is a leper?

I am taking myself out to the drive-in. Yes, they
still exist and have low risk of strangers sitting
next to you and squeezing your knee.

Why I'm Going to Hell

God does not care that I swear when I pray.

Reasons I am Going to Hell

I didn't forward that 'inspirational' bulk email telling me that Jesus will stop loving me if I don't send it to 20 people in the next 10 minutes.

I want to know how many people have been converted by having bible passages yelled at them.

The general sentiment seems to be that if you masturbate, God will condemn you to Hell. I don't think that could possibly be true because why would God condemn you to Hell for something that actually makes you call out to Him?

Baptist Bible camp didn't wash the Catholic off.

True Facts

The Solstice and the Equinox are considered Pagan, but really it's just fucking astronomy.

Though God's path for my life is quite different then God's path for yours, it does not make it wrong.

I thought a man was wearing a white Yarmulke until then I realized he was bald.

It is possible to have a robust spiritual practice and not be a zealot. Try it sometime.

Catholics

If I give up celibacy for Lent, does it count?

The Spanish Inquisition could have done a lot with a potato peeler.

I am going to evening mass because there will be fewer people to punch out there. Peace.

If you forcibly try to separate an Irishman from their Catholicism, all it will get you is blown up.

Churches

I find churches where everyone seems to be just 'going through the motions' incredibly draining.

How disturbing and unfortunate that one runs into so many negative people at church.

I wish the Christian Left would take back theirs churches from those whose God is really money.

Snark Attack

Seriously folks, we all descended from mushrooms.
Get over yourself.

Insults to Try

Most people are jerks. Yes, you.

The Joneses can go screw.

If my language offends you, kindly fuck off.

CRAM IT!!!

Anger

If everyone could stop paying revenge forward
that would be great.

Do you really think being outraged all the time
makes you strong? Try forgiveness.

It is a dangerous truth that most people are
unaware of their own personal addiction to
adrenaline.

Do not allow the ignorant fucks of the world
drag you into circular arguments, in which they
invest so little they can only laugh, and you
invest so much you can only blow a gasket.

Judgment

Your behavior toward me is not a measure of my value as a human being.

If you find amusement in the misfortune of others, please feel free to fuck off now.

Some people's only satisfaction in life is to make others appear and feel 'less than'- but what exactly is less than doing that?

Go to Hell

It should be legal to punch out drunk asshole hecklers.

Everybody get in line! It's ass kicking time!

I feel that anybody that says to me, "tell us how you really feel" can go to hell.

Some people look for any reason to be offended so allow me to provide one: go fuck yourself!

Stupid People

Ever notice that the people who say, "I'm worth it", aren't?

People are stupid and gross. Don't be like people.

Many people seem to want to be able to just 'push a button' when reality demands they actually think.

Pretentious Fucks

You are so fucking hip you need a cane.

Do you think you could try to be a little less full
of shit because I can smell you all the way over
here.

Intellectual arrogance does not prove you are
intelligent; it proves you are a troll.

I know some of you are way cooler than me, so
I wanted to thank you for letting me hang
around the fringe of your ineffable substance.
Look it up.

Substance

If you want to be unique, try being authentic.

Is anyone else fed up with the posturing and drama that is pervasive in our society?

Some people seem to want credit for their intentions without having to actually follow through on them.

I am really sick of living in a society where when you offer a kind word, people assume you are being sarcastic.

Bars & Sex

You know knitting has gone too far
when people are selling yarn in a bar.

Single Woman at the Bar

Hit a new middle age white woman low by bar hopping at the mall.

Yes, it's true. I can sudoku and drink beer at the same time. Thanks for staring.

Exercise class or happy hour?

Overheard: "I'm not showing my tits if that's what you're driving at."

Bar Dating Misfires

Well, I managed to scare off the one guy that shared his beer with me. Typical.

I guess I shouldn't be surprised that I got hit on by drunk vets at the VFW.

I don't miss cigarettes. I miss having an easy way to meet people.

Bar Patrons

Ever notice how stretched and strained smiles on the faces of people in bars are?

Someone threw a beer up in the air and to my surprise I now smell like beer!

True Zen: I can control myself when some trashy broad elbows me in the head.

If someone lights up a cigarette, every other smoker in the vicinity will also light up within five minutes because they are triggered by the initial smoker. This behavior is also true of people checking their phones.

Overdoing It

We need to start calling the Upper Midwest the 'Beer Belly of America'.

Try giving up on drinking Sterno. You might find that most of your problems clear right up.

Remember, if you have to go to work Tuesday morning, DO NOT go out for 2-4-1 beers Monday night.

How Not to Attract a Mate

Guys, please refrain from shaving your chest hair into various shapes because it's weird and not sexy.

Why do some men think that just because THEY are attracted to YOU, you will automatically go out with them?

Hollering at a girl walking down the street from inside the bus you are on is not the way to get a date. Any girl who will let you pick her up this way should be avoided.

Doing It

Can we please get real? All adults really want for Christmas is sex.

Do you think my neighbor's dark haired girlfriend knows about his light haired girlfriend?

If a condom falls off a flaccid dick in the woods, does it make a sound?

It's the start of fucking season (also known as spring) and the animals just go at it without bothering to get a room.

Define: 'low hanging fruit'.

Sex toys

Sex for one counts.

You can tell who's shopping the vegetable aisle for salad and who's trying to get lucky by the way they squeeze the cucumbers.

Videos of powered on vibrators were once considered viable entertainment on the public access channel.

Warning: Sex toys may cause unreasonable expectations.

Dating

The cowards you date refer to this as 'Hanging Out'.
He means his penis.

Dateless Wonder

Went out to dinner with the polar vortex. Best date I've had in years.

I'm either too forward or not forward enough which leads to backwards results.

Just because I do not seem helpless does not mean I do not want help.

Confirmed today: I am too successful, well-rounded, and beautiful to be interested in dating. Uh, what?

Despondent Dating

OK everyone remember- only sexy people deserve happiness.

Listening to people play the dating game makes me wonder why the hell bother.

Do you remember what romance is like? Yeah, me neither.

Just a reminder, your dating relationship should mostly be uplifting, not downtrodden.

I want to know at what age they think women are old enough to not get offended by ads for 'mature singles'.

Dating Nicknames

I understand that you go by the nickname of 'volcano', but I refuse to call you that.

What sort of person attaches 'esquire' to their own name?

When they label themselves 'Thunder from Down Under', what are they referring to? Is it gas? Terrible, terrible gas?

Online Dating

With an online handle like 'nopantiesneeded', I'm not sure why some girl hasn't just snatched you up. NEXT!

The new guy asking for more information about me through my online dating is not interested in pre-marital sex. NEXT!

The fella currently asking for more information about me through online dating can't stand people who use inappropriate humor or have a foul mouth. Well, I'm fucked. NEXT!

Some guy from my online dating site emailed me to specifically ask if I wear pantyhose. NEXT!

Sir Scamalot keeps trying to rescue me through online dating. NEXT!

Mr Right

If you are waiting on an evolved soul... It might be a while...

I need to find a seemingly regular dude that is actually a closet freak (but not too much).

Are you into deep, intelligent, challenging conversation about life, love, and everything?

Mr Wrong

Sorry, I've lost interest because you use the
word 'party' as a verb.

What is with that certain segment of the male
population that feels the need to police the
clothing choices of women?

Is it wrong that I delight in making fools of
men who presume I am less intelligent by virtue
of being female?

I don't care if you have 'spring fever'- go inflict
it on someone else!

There has got to be something between dorky
lonely hearts and whiplash fast men.

What Men Want

Men say they want an honest woman but really, they don't.

If I had a dollar for every man who just stared at my boobs...

Men sure do like pretty girls with style and confidence.

Blow jobs.

What Women Want

Fine food and a good fuck. Is this really a lot to
ask for?

A slow stroll through a field of lavender.

Could someone please point out the location of
'better' so that I may go get the better I am told
I deserve?

Respect and courtesy.

Suggestions on Dating

Who knew that if you actually practice dating you get better at it?

Overheard: 'Well, I'm glad you're over that whole eye candy thing.'

The Kraken may be ugly, but boy does he take dental care seriously.

Tell me your tales and I will tell you mine.

Relationships

Whether you pay it forward or pay it back,
make sure it's only the good stuff.

Break-ups

You would think that a broken heart would be enough to kill you but alas... you live.

It is easier to pack a small bag with a few mementos, switch off the light, and close the door than dig a hole in the backyard.

It is better to lose your pride with someone you love rather than to lose that someone you love with your useless pride.

Mostly, I miss having someone to go get a hot dog with.

Selfishness

You get what you give but some people just take, until you ask them to take out the garbage.

Just because someone doesn't do what you want them to do, does not mean they dislike you, but it might mean they're an asshole.

Not understanding why someone treats you like shit will not prevent them from treating you like shit. It also doesn't mean you deserve it.

Trifling

There are just some people who will hate you for succeeding.

There is a vast difference between tragedy and your disappointed expectations.

Your impatience does not constitute an emergency.

Many people are in the business of creating drama where there is none.

It turns out that no matter how miserable you feel about how some people are, it will not change how some people are.

Remain Vulnerable

Love others and let others love you.

Somehow it is easy to forget how much we matter to others.

Be sure to tell your parents you love them today while you still can.

I thought there was something wrong with me because I could not accept love easily into my life until I realized neither could anyone else.

Authenticity

Show Up. Pay Attention. Tell the Truth. Don't be attached to the results.

Everyone wants to feel like someone cares.

Love is spelled 'T-I-M-E' not 'M-O-N-E-Y'.

If your dog doesn't like someone, believe them. This rule does not apply to your cat.

Others

Life is too short for dipshits.

You may never make a silk purse out of that sow's ear but you need a bunch of creepy worms to make silk and silk tastes terrible fried.

I am turning over a new leaf by using 'thank you' out of context. That should make people uncomfortable enough that they stop talking to me.

Think about how much energy you will save when you not only stop worrying about what other people think but also mind your own damn business!

Writing

Book of Snark: Not as easy as it looks

I, Author

As time goes by, the possibility of me winning a major award seems less and less likely.

Author Bio: sophisticated professional with a fiery passion and the mouth of a sailor.

Why does writing make me want to smash my face into a vat of whipped cream?

If your perception of writers is that they are spooky bookworms, you don't know writers.

The great thing about being a writer is that you can be completely fucking insane and no one questions why.

Career

I probably have no business doing anything but writing for a living, but I also like to eat.

I sincerely wish all I had to do was sit in a coffee shop, read literature, ponder life, and write down my mumblings.

A website promised to reveal the secret of how to become a writer. I wonder how much they are charging to tell people that the true secret is that they have to sit their ass down and actually write.

Fans

I hope that one web crawler from China really enjoyed visiting my blog.

I won some fans today. Burnt out exhaust fans.

I am proud that I can make people laugh out loud and not always at my buffoonery.

Writers don't need a thick skin because of critique... they need it for the indifference.

Not Writing

Please, for the love of God, if you see someone writing, do not sit down next to them and start talking unless you have no other choice.

What kind of monster writes in a library book? In pen?

Do you know what's great about singing? You can do it anywhere. Do you know what's great about writing? Same thing.

Writers Group

I am grateful that my writers' group does not
deteriorate into writer's grope.

Am I too drunk to go to writing class?
Hemingway would not have let it stop him.

Yet another journal has been beaten to death.

Writing Practice

Long hours of quiet, private work unleashed upon the world daily.

I bought a journal at a secondhand bookstore and asked if it was used.

For me, cleaning is a lot like writing; I don't enjoy the process but boy, how about that outcome!

What is writing the book- the dam or the river?

Topics

Writing a book of satire is no joke.

Poetry: the original gateway drug.

Letter writing is a lost art form.

The problem with writing non-fiction stories about one's own life is that you have to relive it.

It has been said that you should write what you know so this year I am publishing a book about an angry middle-aged professional woman who rides the bus.

Word Choice

Yeah, most shit really isn't worth an exclamation point!

I would like a refund on your '$10 dollar' words due to inaccurate usage.

I am plagued by repeated and unnecessary tautology.

With all the slang that ends up actually making it into the Oxford Dictionary, when do you think they are going to make 'shitload' a standard unit of measurement?

Writing Novels

Could I borrow someone's overinflated ego long enough to finish this draft?

I get discouraged and think 'Who will read it?' Then I remember the garbage people pay good money to read.

There are very particular books that I want to read but when I set out to find them in the bookstore it is only then that I realize they are mine.

Life

We do it to ourselves. No, not that.

American Life

The pace of American life is too fast folks. Your SUV can't escape whatever you are running away from.

If the only affirmations you receive come from advertisements, you may wish to consider a change.

Would you like more time in your day, greater peace of mind, and a better quality of life? Turn off your TV.

When did the American Dream become about having a perfect ass?

Quality of Life

Yeah, it turns out that not every day is a 'party'. Seriously, no one has time to fill that many balloons.

Life does not necessarily need to be fun, but it does need to be interesting, but not in the house burnt down sort of way.

If you measure your self-worth by your material wealth, remember that it will all get moldy in the end.

Love and ego are frequently at odds so don't invite them to the same dinner table.

Carpe Diem

It was the best of times, it was the worst of times, at all times.

Waiting around for life to happen is the surest way to have it pass you by.

Most things in life are temporary; some things are just more temporary than others.

Carpe Diem is a fancy way to say get your ass out of bed and stop procrastinating.

We are all stuck in the timeline somewhere. You're not? Does your cereal have a mascot?

Hard Times

It's not just that life goes on. Life must go on.
You must choose to go on.

If you believe a lack of pain is a requirement for
happiness, you will never be happy.

Pretending not to see your problems isn't the
same as pretending not to see people you know
in public.

We all have crushing pain. What we choose to
do in response to it makes us who we are.

How To

Stop trying to make out every word and just hum along.

You do not have to give up control. You have to give up the illusion of control.

Acceptance of reality does not require that I like or approve of it. Take American domestic beer for example.

Do we choose to spend the precious and short time of our lives focused on what is in our power to change or not?

Are you a victim of life or a student of life? There is a vast difference between punishment and discipline unless you are running a marathon which is both.

I Am

If I had any more character I'd be a fucking cartoon.

I, Amazon

When people tell you 'just be yourself' they
don't really mean be your real self.

If I had a dollar for every lie that has been
spoken about what sort of woman I am, I
would be one rich bitch.

Having realistic expectations while maintaining
an ambitious nature is a fine art.

No one is your master except you.

Speak Truth

Throw as many rocks as you like at the truth. They all bounce off.

There is only so long you can shine a cannonball. Whether it is shoddy or shiny eventually you need to just fire it out of the cannon. In either condition it will get the job done.

Send just $19.99 and we'll send you important information on how to get rich by telling people what they want to hear!

Sell a fool the notion that he is not foolish, and he will pledge his allegiance to your lies.

Social Reject

I have way too much personality for this planet.

I am not hip despite the fact that I have two of them.

I was processed in a facility that also processes nuts.

Bad Attitude

So, if I'm not happy and I know it- what do I do?

I'm sure I cared but I can't remember when.

I am in a mood and, as with all weather, must wait for it to pass.

I want to return my life for a refund.

Get it Done

Whatever it is, I'm doing it the Jack LaLanne way!

Just because you find it difficult does not excuse you from dealing with it.

I may fear or dislike my choices, but I at least do have them.

Being unable should never be confused with being unwilling.

How much of your life are you going to waste waiting on others to live up to your expectations?

Self Esteem

Not even oafs like to feel like they are an oaf.

Arrogance and self-confidence are not the same thing.

Love from another cannot and will not ever replace love of the self.

Self-hatred is the root of all evil.

Self-Care

Self-care is reason enough.

Self-control works wonders. Try some this weekend!

Forgive people- not for their benefit, for you own.

If you want to change the world, start with the internal one.

Our Place

The real tragedy in life is not when darkness falls- that is just the reality of existence. No, the real tragedy is to see the light places between the dark ones but not believe that you belong there and so in the darkness remain.

It often feels like we are fighting others, but the truth is that we are mostly fighting ourselves.

Your zip code does not determine your value as a human being.

Once you figure out that you are no worse than anyone, you will stop trying to prove you are better than everyone.

Be brave enough to tell your stories to the world, especially if they're funny.

Congratulations!
You made it to the end of the Book of Snark!

Did you love this book?
Please help others to enjoy it-
- Write a review on Amazon!
- Tell your family and friends!
- Donate it to the Little Library in your neighborhood!

Did you hate this book?
Please help others to be annoyed by it-
- Give it to your enemies!
- Make it a stocking stuffer for your mother-in-law!
- Leave an anonymous copy in the staff lunchroom!

And remember…

Book of Snark makes a great regift!

Acknowledgments

Loren Niemi, my ever-ready editor and cheerleader. Thank you for sharing your life with me.

Alexander Niece, my cover designer. Sorry I dragged you into this.

Jennifer Haehnel, my beta reader. Thank you for your contributions and assuring me this book doesn't suck.

Minneapolis Metro Transit, #113. Thank you for putting up with this angry professional woman all these years.

Bill Mounts, my father. Thank you for letting my sisters name me.

Mary Mounts, my mother. Thank you for the end.

About the Author

Christine (Tension) Mounts gave up trying to be a serious writer and decided to play to her strengths.

Book of Snark is her first published work of satire.

She lives in Minneapolis with two sweet kitties and one Kool Kat.

You can read her blog, such as it is, at cmmounts.com.

Made in the USA
Monee, IL
12 October 2020